52 WOMEN OF WHATCOM

THE LEAGUE OF WOMEN VOTERS OF BELLINGHAM/WHATCOM COUNTY

To request permissions, contact the publisher at
publishing@villagebooks.com

Paperback: 978-0-9842389-8-9
Library of Congress Number: 2020917443

First paperback edition September 2020.

RESEARCH AND WRITING
Cascadia Weekly: Kate Kershner, lead;
Marian Exall, Jayne Freudenberger, Elsie Heinrick,
Elaine Hormal, Linda Lambert, Jane Lowry,
Donita Reams, Judith Wiseman.

LEAD EDITORS
Jayne Freudenberger and Linda Lambert

DESIGN AND LAYOUT
Chelanne Evans

OVERSIGHT
Jill Bernstein, Chair of Centennial Committee

Printed in the USA by Village Books.

Village Books & Paper Dreams
1200 11th St
Bellingham, WA 98225

villagebooks.com

WITH SPECIAL THANKS TO

Cascadia Weekly and Village Books

PHOTOS PROVIDED BY
Jeff Jewell, Research Technician, Whatcom Museum of Art and History
Tamara Belts, Special Collections Manager, WWU
Robert Clark, MGF Digital Video Services, WWU
Members of the League of Women Voters

PROOFREADING AND BIBLIOGRAPHY BY
Lisa Dailey of Sidekick Press

RESEARCH AND BACKGROUND INFORMATION FROM
Lynne Masland's book:
*100 Years of Challenge and Change: Whatcom Women
and the Bellingham YWCA*

52 WOMEN OF WHATCOM

TABLE OF CONTENTS

INTRODUCTION. 9

EARLY DAYS

Phoebe Judson 12
Sisters Teresa Moran & Stanislaus Tighe 13
Ida Agnes Baker 14
Ella Higginson 15
Frances Larrabee 16
Helen Loggie 17
Frances Axtell 18
Mabel Zoe Wilson 19
Bess Bay 20
Nellie Duff 21
Catherine Montgomery 22
Dolly Connelly 23
The Aftermath Club 24

TAKING UP THE BATON

Violet Hillaire 28
Lois Garlick 29
Claire vg Thomas 30
Catherine May 31
Mary Robinson 32
Anne Brown 33
Bess Christman 34
Ramona (Hi-olit-saw) Phare-Morris 35
Dorothy (Dotty) Dale 36
Carol Batdorf 37
Noémi Ban 38
Catherine Tally 39
The YWCA, Bellingham Chapter 40

CONTINUING THE TRADITION

Julie Foster 44
Peggy Zoro 45
Karen W. Morse 46
Phyllis Self 47
JoAnn Roe-Hubbard 48
Mary Kay Becker 49
Chris Paul 50
Harriet Spanel 51
Catharine (Kitty) Stimpson 52
Joan Beardsley 53
Lynda Goodrich 54
Shirley Osterhaus 55
Noriko Lao 56
Juanita Jefferson 57

LOOKING TOWARD THE FUTURE

Dorie Belisle 60
Kathi Hiyane-Brown 61
Raquel Montoya-Lewis 62
Kelli Linville 63
Sue Sharpe 64
Pat Rose 65
Deborra Garrett 66
Rosalinda Guillen 67
Mauri Ingram 68
Flo Simon 69
Janet Marino 70
League of Women Voters 71

PHOTOGRAPH CREDITS 73
BIBLIOGRAPHY 83

INTRODUCTION

The League of Women Voters of Bellingham/Whatcom's Centennial team began the 52 Women of Whatcom project to bring attention to the talents, expertise, and gifts women have contributed to our community. For each week of our centennial year and the hundredth anniversary year of suffrage, we chose a local woman to honor and represent our community. White, black, or brown, these honorees met the challenges they faced with courage, whether it was climbing that mountain, lobbying before Congress for native rights, starting a library from scratch, or challenging their place in politics.

Representing diversity in age, era, and race, as well as different areas of concern—social services, the arts, politics, education, etc.—each would tell you she did not do her work alone. Some worked behind the scenes, others led from the front. All gave what they could: blankets to those who were cold, skills and confidence to young people, paintings that reflected the beauty of the Northwest.

We are also honoring three organizations representing many more women who worked to make our community the oft-cited "best place to live." We hope readers will feel as proud as we are when meeting them on our pages.

We are grateful for *Cascadia Weekly*'s generous offer to honor one woman each week in print and online and Village Books' enthusiastic offer to publish our updated material in book form. 52 Women of Whatcom is a fitting capstone to our year-long celebration of the 100th anniversary of the first great victory for suffrage. We do recognize that women of color were still denied the opportunity to vote for many decades. The battle is never-ending to keep and expand our original victory. The League of Women Voters, 100 years old this year, begins the new century by rededicating itself to championing not only voting rights, but equal opportunities to thrive for all American citizens.

EARLY DAYS

PHOEBE JUDSON

1831–1926

This "Pioneer Wife" was forward thinking on women's rights.

Phoebe Judson is acknowledged as the first non-native woman to settle in the Lynden area. The mother of four biological children and eleven adopted children, she became known as the "Mother of Lynden." She supported women's suffrage and the right of women to own property long before either came to pass. In 1853, she and her husband, Holden Judson, and their young family traveled by covered wagon on the Overland Trail from Ohio to Puget Sound in the Washington Territory. The Judsons arrived at the mouth of the Nooksack by shovel-nosed canoe around 1870. Phoebe Judson was soon called "Aunt Phoebe," someone you went to whether you needed a pail of buttermilk or childbirth help. In 1874, they turned their home into the local post office. Judson is credited with giving Lynden its name, derived from the poem "Hohenlinden" by Thomas Campbell. In the 1870s, she described her life in frequent letters

to the *Bellingham Bay Mail.* In 1886, she organized the construction of the Northwest Normal School later renamed Washington State Normal School. Judson is the author of *A Pioneer's Search for an Ideal Home*, first published in 1925.

SISTERS TERESA MORAN &
STANISLAUS TIGHE

(dates unknown)

Two young nuns with only three months of medical training begin Bellingham's hospital.

Sisters Teresa Moran and Stanislaus Tighe of the New Jersey Catholic order, Sisters of St. Joseph of Peace, came to Bellingham in 1890. Responding to the desperate need for hospitals in the Northwest, the young sisters boarded a train whose final destination was Fairhaven. Upon arrival, they immediately set out to build a hospital. Prominent businessman J.J. Donovan met with them three days after their arrival to start the planning and fundraising. Donovan and friends decided to solicit funds from Whatcom County residents. The sisters traveled to the lumber camps and outlying districts selling tickets—an early form of health insurance. For a payment of $10, a lumberjack received an elegantly printed paper allowing him admission to the hospital (as yet unbuilt) for one year. The first St. Joseph Hospital, constructed in three months, was a small two-story frame building on South Hill with room for about thirty patients. Sisters Teresa and Stanislaus were joined by four more sisters and, in January 1891, the hospital opened to patients.

The system they created eventually grew to more than five hospitals. The order relinquished day-to-day management in the 1970s, but the hospitals remain a Catholic health system under lay leadership.

IDA AGNES BAKER

1859–1921

Baker wrote "Elizabeth Cady Stanton and Her Work," an article published in the June 1899 issue of National Suffrage Bulletin.

Born in Iowa, Ida Agnes Baker began her lifelong work for women's suffrage at Central Iowa College, where she earned bachelor's and master's degrees. In 1899, she became one of the nine founding faculty members of Bellingham Normal School (Western Washington University), teaching forestry, grammar, and music. Besides teaching, she was an early environmentalist, writer, and local leader in the women's suffrage movement, helping women in Washington State achieve the right to vote in 1910, a decade before the nation granted it. Baker helped organize the Bellingham chapter of the Women's Good Government League, a national group devoted to promoting reform and combating political corruption. In a 1919 article, she recounted a ten-day hike with thirteen female students to Mt. Baker, believed to be the first such all-woman hiking trip in the area. In 1900, Baker and her friend, Catherine Montgomery, joined forces to help found the Progressive, Literary and Fraternal Club, an organization dedicated to the political influence of women. In January 1921, after attending a meeting of The League of Women Voters, she was struck by a streetcar at the corner of Laurel and Garden streets and died. In 2008, Baker was awarded the YWCA Northwest Women's Hall of Fame Legacy Award.

ELLA HIGGINSON

1861–1940

Her most popular poem, "Four Leaf Clover," was set to music and was the official song of the National Federation of Women's Clubs.

Ella Higginson, a writer of short stories, novels, travel articles, and verse, was the first Poet Laureate of Washington State. Higginson was born in Council Grove, Kansas. Her family fled pre-Civil War "Bloody Kansas," and traveled across the country by oxcart to Oregon, where, at fourteen, she published her first poem in the *Oregon City Enterprise* newspaper. In 1885, she married Russell Higginson. They settled in Bellingham in 1888, opened a drugstore in Fairhaven, and built a house on Sehome Hill. She wrote for local newspapers as well as national magazines. *McClure's* and *Collier's* awarded her first prizes for her stories. MacMillan published five books of her poems and fiction. *The New York Times* praised her poetry collection *When the Birds Go North Again* (1902) for its "depth and delicacy of feeling." During the First World War, Higginson was a volunteer with the Bellingham branch of the American Red Cross and received the Red Cross Medal for her service. A strong supporter of the arts, education, and women's rights, she helped establish Bellingham's first library and was campaign manager for Frances Axtell's election to Washington State's House of Representatives.

FRANCES LARRABEE

1867–1941

She believed in women's suffrage and equal opportunities for women in education and society.

Frances Larrabee was a prominent civic leader and club member in early Bellingham. Born in Missouri, she was an accomplished pianist who studied at major music conservatories on the East Coast and in Berlin. After marrying, she and her husband, C. X. Larrabee, moved to the Northwest, where they lived in his Fairhaven hotel for over twenty years, raising their family there. As they were building a new home in Edgemoor, C. X. Larrabee died suddenly. Undeterred, Frances took over the construction project and joined the management of his company, Pacific Reality.

Larrabee was passionate about those less fortunate, and funded the Bellingham Bay Home for Children, a safe haven for homeless children. She was active in the Presbyterian Church and donated the property upon which two church buildings were erected. Upon joining the Monday Club—the oldest literary club in this area—she transformed the club into an organization that highlighted societal and political issues of the Progressive Era. Her most well-known project is the YWCA building on Forest Street. Through her civic work and commitment to social causes, Larrabee was a powerful influence in Whatcom County.

HELEN LOGGIE

1895–1976

*"I'm a Northwest artist, and the cathedrals of
the Northwest are the trees."*

Helen Loggie was a local artist who gained international acclaim for her etchings of trees and coastlines. Born to a Bellingham lumber baron, Loggie left Whatcom County for the East Coast. After graduating from Smith College, she moved to New York to study at the Arts Student League from 1916 to 1924 where she developed her own style. School luminaries included Norman Rockwell and Jackson Pollock. Loggie toured Europe for two years where she created an extensive body of sketches. There she met painter John Taylor Arms, beginning a twenty-five-year collaboration. She returned home to the Northwest to draw and paint the forests, mountains, and island shores. In the 1930s, she supported Western Washington University's new Studio Gallery with advice and by bringing quality art shows to the college. Whenever she arrived at the harbor to sketch the ship "Vigilant," men at the dock put her up in the hoist, where she sat, sketching. Her work has been exhibited abroad and collected by such institutions as the Library of Congress, Glasgow University, and the British Museum. In 1957, she was named an academician by the National Academy of Design. Numerous prints and drawings reside in the collection at the WWU Gallery of Art.

Frances Axtell

1866–1953

"Most men are in politics because they want to do something...whereas women are in it because they want to get something done."

B orn in Illinois and educated in a one-room school, Axtell earned a doctorate from DePauw University at age twenty-three. She moved to Lynden, taught at their Normal School, then traveled in Europe for a year. She and Dr. William Axtell married in 1891 in Illinois, relocating to New Whatcom (Bellingham) in 1894. From 1902 to 1942, the Axtells lived at 413 E. Maple. She employed the wood-carving skills she learned in Germany to construct the house's staircase panels. Axtell

was the first president of the New Whatcom Ladies Cooperative Society and a charter member of the Aftermath Club. She successfully worked to restore the right to vote that women had from 1883 to 1888 in Washington Territory. Axtell and Nena Croake of Tacoma were the first two women to serve in Washington State's House of Representatives. Named Sevilla at birth, during her campaign, she thought "Frances" (her daughter's name) would be more familiar to voters. Axtell served from 1913 to 1915, promoting minimum wage and public safety legislation. She was known as "the lady from Whatcom who votes as she pleases." In 1917, President Woodrow Wilson appointed her vice-chair of the Employees' Compensation Commission, the first woman selected for a federal commission.

MABEL ZOE WILSON

1878–1964

Her dream was that the library would serve as the "students' workshop" where they could "double and magnify their creative work."

M abel Zoe Wilson was the librarian who created a library for what became Western Washington University. Wilson had no formal library training, but she arranged a few piles of magazines and 400–500 books into an organized collection in a study hall, created a handwritten catalog, and began teaching students how to access the library and its resources. Wilson was born in Athens, Ohio. In 1909, she got her library degree in New York from the school founded by Melvil Dewey himself. Why she came west for a salary of $600 a year is not known, but within a year there were 4,600 books properly catalogued. In 1924, WWU built a new library. She developed the library's holdings, secured additional professional and clerical staff, and expanded the library's instructional services to include credit courses in library and research skills. Wilson

served on many state, regional, and national library committees, including the one tasked with forming the Washington Library Association. She was beloved by students and faculty and famous for the extravagant parties she held for them. In 1964, these friends campaigned successfully for the library's name change to the Mabel Zoe Wilson Library.

BESS BAY

1898–1998

Bess Bay was instrumental in the formation of Whatcom Community College.

Born in Missouri, Bess Bay earned a BS in Education and an MA in Education and the Practical Arts from Columbia University. She married Captain John Bay and they lived in Washington, DC, for nine busy years which included receptions twice a year at the White House. When World War II began, Bay worked in the Red Cross office. Though she and her husband enjoyed DC, finding people friendly, they moved west to Whatcom County in 1949 where her husband grew up. "We liked living in Lynden and the unhurried life here," she said. Her "unhurried life" included support of the arts and education earning her the moniker "Grand Dame of Lynden" and a street name: Bess Bay Drive. Her influence stretched beyond Lynden. In 1969, Governor Dan Evans appointed her to the first board of trustees for Whatcom Community College (WCC) which was committed to "borrow, rent, lease, or rebuild facilities, but not create a central campus." She served a term as chair of the board of trustees for the "campus without walls."

NELLIE DUFF

1897–1971

She had 100 hours of flight time—enough, she said, to steer but not to land a plane.

Nellie Duff began her career as a reporter in Sangamon County, Illinois, where she compiled *The Honor Book of Sangamon County* 1917–1919, a 1,200-page volume that recognized most of the county's World War I military veterans and home-front supporters. She wrote silent film screenplays and was editor of the Automobile Association of America's flight magazine. In 1935, she moved to Bellingham and worked for the *Bellingham Herald* for twenty-five years. As the newly elected president of the International Peace Arch Association, Duff invited President Eisenhower to the Association's peace summit in 1955. He declined but sent Nelson Rockefeller. Retiring in 1960, Duff continued her work on peace projects and student exchange programs. The International Peace Arch was erected in 1921 on the US/Canadian border. In 1964, "Boundaries not Barriers" was the theme of Peace Arch events and the 75th anniversary of Washington state-hood. Duff scheduled a 1,110-passenger train to bring people from Seattle and invited the children on the train to march in the opening parade and partic-ipate in the flag exchange with Canadian children. Duff was elected president of the International Peace Arch Association sever-al times in the 1950s and 1960s.

CATHERINE MONTGOMERY

1867–1957

Montgomery is known as the "Mother of the Pacific Coast Trail"

Catherine Montgomery was a thirty-two-year-old single woman when she accepted a teaching position for what was to become Western Washington University. As a dauntless outdoorswoman, she and her friend, Ida Baker, loved "tramping" on the mountain trails. When Baker died unexpectedly, Montgomery wrote a eulogy for her friend called "Tramping Together." In 1906, she joined forty-seven bloomer-wearing women as they attempted to climb Mt. Baker's northwest face. In 1926, she showed pictures of the

Appalachian Trail to Seattle mountaineer Joseph Hazard and suggested the creation of a similar trail with shelters and mile markers on the West Coast. Hazard took the idea to Bellingham's Mt. Baker Club and other hiking groups and today the Pacific Coast Trail is 2,650 miles long, attracting thousands of hikers each year. Montgomery was also a homesteader, a leader in the 1890s women's club movement, a suffragist, an educator of teachers, and a philan-

thropist. When she retired in 1926, her annual salary was $32,000, but she left an estate worth $1 million in today's dollars, which she gifted to a State Forest Preserve near Enumclaw. Thousands of children visit the Catherine Montgomery Interpretive Center each year.

DOLLY CONNELLY

1913–1995

In the 1950s and 1960s, the Pacific Northwest was a hotbed of industry-vs.-conservancy arguments, and Connelly was involved in all of them.

Dolly Connelly worked as a photographer and journalist for publications including *Time, Life,* and *Sports Illustrated.* With respect to sports magazines, she believed that they should cover more than "sweaty sock sports." From her home in Bellingham, Connelly wrote about, photographed— and became a fierce advocate for—environmental issues in the Northwest. She covered the potential environmental ramifications of a proposed open pit copper mine at Glacier Peak Wilderness in the 1960s. A 'Spit on Your Open Pit' bumper sticker graced the Connelly Plymouth station wagon. She pressed for the formation of the North Cascades National Park. In 1960, Connelly's photo of Bellingham Bay—its murky waters polluted by pulp mill runoff—accompanied an early *Life* article about the environment. In 1965, she climbed the 14,000 ft. Mt. Kennedy in the Yukon with Robert Kennedy and Jim Whitaker. Her subsequent piece included an account of the journey and the ruminations of Kennedy on his slain brother. Connelly's legacy continues to promote environmental journalism and awareness. Her son, *Seattle Post-Intelligencer* columnist Joel Connelly, set up a foundation to support the annual Dolly Connelly Award for Excellence in Environmental Journalism to small and midsize newspapers in the Pacific Northwest Newspaper Association.

THE AFTERMATH CLUB

1895–2003

A major influence on community life for 107 years.

The Aftermath Club, organized in 1895 by twelve young women of New Whatcom, began as The Aftermath Reading Circle, a literary and social club. The name was chosen to indicate "a second gleaning." The women wrote a constitution, bylaws, and an annual agenda of study and presentations on a wide range of topics. They also raised money for the new YMCA and local agencies. In later years, they donated scholarships for Western Washington University students. When the reading circle became the formal Aftermath Club, members decided to build a clubhouse. Built in 1904, it was the first women's clubhouse in Washington state. The Italian-villa style, rare in the Northwest, reflected the group's lofty cultural ambitions. Remarkably, the women financed and paid off the debt to their property while continuing their charitable work. They even offered an annual prize for the most improved lawn. After the sale of the building in 1977, members continued to sponsor programs until the club's dissolution in 2003. The building remains today as Broadway Hall. The Aftermath Club women, too numerous to honor all by name, were a presence of civility and social progress in Bellingham.

TAKING UP THE BATON

VIOLET HILLAIRE

1930–1995

"Don't bother to come home if you didn't vote."

Violet Hillaire was an advocate for Indian health and education. Born on Portage Island at a time when there was neither running water nor health care, she attended Lummi Day School, completing her education at Salem's Chemawa Indian School. At twenty-three, she married Henry Hillaire. They parented fourteen children resulting in thirty-one grandchildren and thirty-one great-grandchildren to date. As a vice chair of the Northwest Portland Area Indian Health Board, she is credited with helping to shape the board's mission to eliminate health disparities and improve the delivery of culturally-appropriate, high-level health care to Northwest tribes. She worked with Lummi leader Sam Cagey, Sr., whom she described as "a warrior for Indian people" and as "one who would go down fighting," a spirit she herself exhibited. Family members

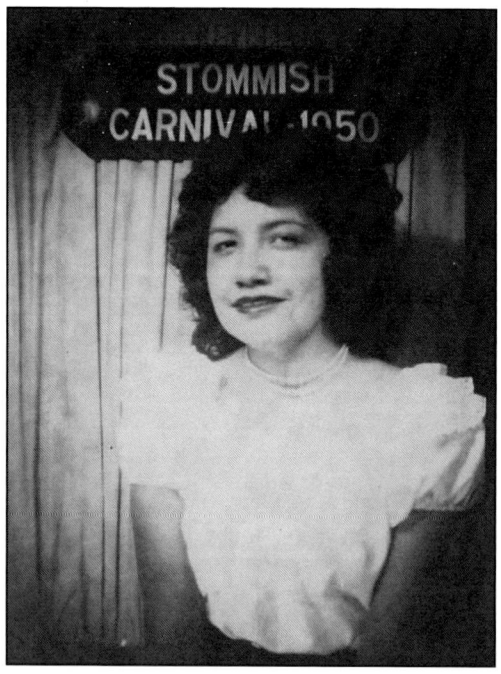

remember her transporting voters to the polls and, with other unpaid lobbyists, cramming into a single hotel room in DC to support the needs of her tribe. She distributed blankets to those who were cold. She told her children and grandchildren: "When you do anything, do it from your heart, and do it for your people."

Lois Garlick

1920–2015

Garlick's early, effective, and action-oriented stewardship is a model for today's environmental movements.

Lois Garlick was an environmental activist. Born and raised in Seattle, she earned a degree in zoology from the University of Washington. While working at Western Washington University, she met and married her husband George. They shared the same passions: science, boating, and conservation. Her legacy of environmental civic activities included helping create the North Cascades Audubon Society chapter, leading the Clean Water Alliance, and saving Bellingham's Scudder Pond from development. Lois and George were stewards for Chuckanut Island, keeping it safe for birds. Garlick ran Raptor's Roost, a bird rehabilitation care center tending to wounded birds from pigeons to barn owls to hawks. She was instrumental in passing the Shoreline Management Act and was a frequent contributor to *Whatcom Watch*. The Garlicks were also involved in work with the Huxley College of Environmental Science and the Institute for Freshwater Studies. In 2004, both received the Environmental Heroes Award by RE Sources. At age

87, Garlick filed for county executive and campaigned vigorously across the county. She ran because no one else would oppose the popular incumbent. Though she did not win, she captured a sizable number of votes.

CLAIRE VG THOMAS

1917–2008

Thomas was called Lynden's "Matron of the Arts."

Claire vg Thomas of Lynden, Washington, was a nationally-known choir director, pianist, and organist whose life revolved around her passion for music. She attended the Washington State Normal School in Bellingham that became WWU, then went on to receive bachelor and master's degrees from Northwestern University in Illinois. She toured the US as a concert pianist and organ recitalist, later traveling around the world several times on a major cruise ship. After marrying William Thomas in Lynden, they moved to New York State where she raised their family. She was an audition accompanist for Rogers and Hammerstein. Serving as the Minister of Music at the Scarsdale Congregational Church for twenty years, she played the organ and directed six choirs. After returning to Lynden in 1972, Thomas became a community leader, patron, and benefactor of the arts and music. A founder of the Lynden Pioneer Museum and the Whatcom Symphony

Orchestra (now Bellingham Symphony Orchestra), she chaired Lynden's Centennial Celebration as part of the national Bicentennial. Thomas founded and led the Queen Julianna Theater in Lynden. In 2001, the Lynden Performing Arts Guild renamed it the Claire vg Thomas Theater to honor Thomas' dedication to music and the arts.

CATHERINE MAY

1916–2003

May was a friend and advocate to seniors and those with disabilities.

Catherine May dedicated her life to helping others by serving on the Bellingham School Board, working with the Bellingham YWCA, and directing the Whatcom County Senior Services. The Catherine May Apartments for seniors and persons with disabilities, owned by the Whatcom Council on Aging, testifies to her hard work. At various times, she was the president of the League of Women Voters, the Aftermath Club, and the American Association of University Women. She also served as an elected Bellingham School Director for fifteen years and as chair for services to disabled children for the Washington State School Directors' Association. In the 1950s and 1960s, May led the Y-Teens Group for the YWCA and organized a program for young married women with toddlers. As director of Whatcom County Senior Services, she procured the first state and federal grants for senior health care, nutrition assistance, housing, and transportation. She oversaw the construction of the first Whatcom County Senior Center and in 1981 was a delegate to the National White House Conference on Aging.

MARY ROBINSON

1927–2020

She was at the forefront of changes for Western's university women by implementing Title IX.

Mary Robinson was appointed Dean of Women at Western Washington University in 1969 after having held a similar position at the American University of Beirut in Lebanon. In 1972, Title IX was passed prohibiting sex discrimination in educational institutions receiving federal funding. During her tenure at WWU, Robinson oversaw and led those sweeping changes in university education for women. She initiated and managed WWU's first affirmative action program for minorities. She established daycare services for students, the host family program for foreign students, and summer courses for school children and high school seniors. In the mid-1970s, she organized brown bag lunch discussions at the YWCA to address emerging environmental and women's issues. Robinson, who was elected YWCA board president in 1972, also served for many years on the board of the United Way of Whatcom County. In 1987, she became the second woman inducted into the Bellingham Rotary Club. As a life-long supporter of the YWCA and its board president, she served on their advisory board of trustees well into the 2000s. Even after retirement, Robinson continued to contribute her wisdom and experience, including work on a task force to review and expand the United Way's non-discrimination policy in 2000.

ANNE BROWN

1926–2018

Prior to Brown's work, families often had to institutionalize their developmentally disabled children.

Anne Brown was a public health nurse and long-time advocate for children with developmental delays in Whatcom County. Brown earned her nursing degree at Adelphi College in 1947. She worked in 1948 for the Public Health Department at Seattle Well Child Clinic and Harborview Hospital nursing polio patients. Brown arrived in Bellingham in 1966 and started working for Whatcom County Public Health managing a program for families of young children with developmental delays. In 1968, she helped create the Whatcom Association of Training Centers Inc. which served as the first special education preschool. Eventually, an infant-toddler special needs program, Whatcom Center for Early Learning, was developed, and in 1971 Brown started the Coalition for Child Advocacy. She received The Giraffe Award (1987) "for people who stick their necks out" from a local radio station, the Whatcom County Peace Builder Award from Whatcom Dispute Resolution Center (2003),

and she was inducted into the Northwest Women's Hall of Fame in 1999. Each year, Brown attended an event important to her family—a celebration of April 16, 1939, the date her family arrived at Ellis Island from Nazi Germany.

BESS CHRISTMAN

1924–2016

A student scholarship program at Western honors the Christmans.

Bess Christman and her husband, Bob, believed in the power of education and in the importance of community. They adopted, loved, and raised four children. When her husband began teaching in 1960 and went on to chair the geology department at WWU, Christman put her energies to work for the community. Bess, a member of Sacred Heart Catholic Church, was a board member of the Interfaith Coalition and a founding mother of Lydia Place—a transitional home for women and children. She served on the board of trustees for the Whatcom Volunteer Center. Other interests included Catholic Community Services, the Volunteer Chore Program, Opportunity Council, Northwest Regional Council, Maple Alley Inn, American Association of University Women, and Church Women United. In 2000, she was inducted into the Northwest Women's Hall of Fame. That same year, Mayor Mark Asmundson named her the Citizen of the Year. When there was a call for service Bess answered it.

RAMONA (HI-OLIT-SAW) PHARE-MORRIS

1931–2018

Because of her extensive knowledge of water rights, Morris was an effective advocate for her tribe on critical issues to her community.

Ramona (Hi-olit-saw) Phare-Morris grew up on the Lummi Reservation and later served as director of the Lummi Health Clinic and chair of the Law and Order Committee. Morris was a member of the Lummi Tribal Council and assisted in developing Lummi aquaculture. She believed that salmon were sacred, placed in the waters of the Salish Sea for the tribe's use—Lummi's Sche'lang'en or way of life. She was on the Lummi Task Force Against Taxation and was appointed chair of the Indian Advisory Committee. Morris gathered witnesses to testify in the Boldt case and lobbied and garnered federal support from members of Congress. Her knowl-

edge of water rights and her ability to persuade and inform prompted the other side to accuse her of being an attorney. She always encouraged tribes to work together on common issues. As a leader she was driven by her commitment to the children and to the Lummi community, striving for everyone to receive services without limitation. Morris was inducted into the Northwest Women's Hall of Fame in 2014.

Dorothy (Dotty) Dale

1925–2020

Her church's political action group is still known as The Dotty Dale Women's Circle.

Dorothy Dale met her husband, Al, while attending Chicago Theological Seminary. They married in 1948 and spent their life together in the peace and justice movement. In 1955, they moved to Bellingham where Dale served as interim director and board president of the YWCA. She started a pre-school and taught parent/children classes at the Lummi Nation. Moving to Chicago, Dale earned a Master of Religious Education and taught school on Chicago's  south side, after which the couple left to work with Global Ministry in Fiji and Poland. The family retired to Bellingham in 1990. Dale became a familiar figure at the Friday Peace Vigil and was instrumental in the establishment of the Rainbow Coalition. In 2002, Dale gave startup funding to help found the Whatcom County Peace and Justice Center. She was elected its first president. She belonged to Jobs with Justice and was an ally of the Lummi Nation. Both Dale and her husband received the Whatcom Peace and Justice Lifetime Peacemakers Award in 2006 and the Jobs with Justice Workers' Rights Champions Award in 2007. Dale was inducted into the YWCA Northwest Women's Hall of Fame in 2012.

CAROL BATDORF

1919–1995

Batdorf studied and taught about Coast Salish traditions.

Carol Batdorf was an author, artist, and educator who taught and wrote about Coast Salish people and traditions. Born in St. Paul, Minnesota, Batdorf moved to Bellingham in 1927. During WWII she served in U.S. Naval Intelligence. An instructor in First Nation Studies at WWU, she learned to design and carve totem poles and weave baskets. Her passion was Northwest Indian art. Some of her artistic efforts were displayed in 1995 at Lake Tennant Park in Ferndale and in the Intalco Aluminum Corporation's totem logo. Her strong interest in the Coast Salish people led to service on the staff of the Lummi Community Action program on the Lummi Reservation. She was district director for Camp Fire Girls and active in introducing girls to Coast Salish history. Her book *Northwest Native Harvest* focuses on Coast

Salish food gathering and preparation, emphasizing the close relationship between food and culture. She also wrote children's books and coloring books about Coast Salish life.

Noémi Ban

1922–2019

"Life is precious. Life is wonderful. I love life. I do not hate. If I would have hate in me right now, I would be the prisoner of my own hate, and I want to be free."

Noémi Ban and her family were living in the town of Debrecen, Hungary, when the Nazis invaded in March 1944. Noémi, her mother, grandmother, sister, and baby brother were forced into a cramped cattle car and transported to Auschwitz-Birkenau. Ban was among a thousand women who worked as slave laborers in a munition factory at Allendorf and one of twelve women to escape the women's death march in early 1945. She and  her father were the only family members to survive the Holocaust. Later, Noémi and her husband and children escaped oppression in Soviet Hungary. They settled in St. Louis, Missouri, in 1957. Ban learned English, earned a degree in education, and became a teacher. In the 1990s, Noémi's family moved to Bellingham where she began her public speaking career on the Holocaust. Ban co-authored *Sharing is Healing: A Holocaust Survivor's Story*, and co-founded the Northwest Center for Holocaust, Genocide and Ethnocide Education at WWU. Ban received honorary doctorates from Gonzaga University and Western Washington University, and became a regular speaker in local schools and organizations. She was posthumously honored by WWU's creation of a minor in Holocaust and Genocide Studies, making it the first public university in the state to offer such a program.

CATHERINE TALLY

1926–2003

She campaigned for seniors and native rights at the highest level of government.

Catherine Tally was an education activist and Lummi Nation leader. With her six children she traveled across the states following her husband's naval career. Starting as a welder in the shipyards at Bremerton in the 1940s, Tally taught that skill in South Carolina when soldiers came home from the war. When she returned to the place of her birth, the Lummi Nation, she used her experience for the benefit of her community, welding the floodgates for the Lummi Aquaculture project and backstops for baseball fields. Passionate about education, Tally earned a college degree and was Lummi Education Coordinator as well as a member of the Elders' Advisory Committee for the Lummi Tribal School. She campaigned for senior citizens' programs and lobbied Lummi leadership and state and federal governments for the Little Bear Creek Elder Apartments. She received local and national recognition for her work. In 1992, the American Association of Retired Persons desig-

nated her as a national minority affairs spokesperson. The Volunteer Center celebrated her efforts to promote literacy through the Grandparents' Brigade at the Lummi School. She was also honored by the Northwest Women's Hall of Fame.

The YWCA, Bellingham Chapter

founded 1907

The YWCA mission is to empower women and eliminate racism.

Housed in the handsome Georgian building built by the Larrabee family in 1915, the YWCA continues to serve their mission of eliminating racism and empowering women. The women belonging to YWCA have given to this community for over 100 years; It was impossible to choose just one to represent the organization and the roles throughout the century.

At present, they provide housing and support services for women in transition. Rentals from the lovely main floor ballroom and kitchen help supply revenue. The basement holds the Lillian Hellman Back to Work Boutique. Previously, the organization has supported Traveler's Aid, Girl Reserves, Moms and Tots, swimming lessons, Y Teens, Y Wives, and the Sunset Club for seniors. By 1969, over 10,888 women and girls had participated.

As a more social justice emphasis evolved, the YWCA served as an incubator for Women in Trades, eco action (sparking the acquisition of land for Boulevard Park), GED options, rape relief, Crisis line, Jail alternatives, encore for breast cancer survivors, and the other bank. Their mission now is to serve single women who have no place to go because of financial issues or violence against them. Testimony from previous residents describe the YWCA as a haven where they found the space and support to move to productive lives.

CONTINUING THE TRADITION

JULIE FOSTER

1945–2016

The renovation of the YWCA led a change from providing ongoing housing to providing emergency and transitional housing.

Julie Foster was an active volunteer in Bellingham who entered leadership positions in several local organizations. Foster was born in Seattle and worked in advertising but dedicated herself to serving the community after moving to Bellingham in 1980. She was a charter member and president of the Bellingham City Club, as well as a founder of the Northwest Women's Hall of Fame. Foster is credited with developing the Bellingham Public Library logo and was a longtime member of the Bellingham Rotary Club and Bellingham Soroptimists chapter. After serving as president of the YWCA Board of Directors, in 1998, Foster became the executive director of the YWCA at a perilous time for the agency. She led successful fundraising efforts and managed the $1.6 million renovation of the building. She expanded the Back to Work Boutique and changed the direction of the mission to transitional housing. Despite a diagnosis of multiple sclerosis, Foster remained at the helm of the YWCA until 2011, accepting her disease with dignity, continuing to mentor women and lead the organization with wisdom and love.

PEGGY ZORO

b. 1942

Many area nonprofits have benefitted from Zoro's business acumen.

Peggy Zoro's efforts combined her success in business and nonprofit management with her long-time interest in education to improve the lives of people in Whatcom County. A former teacher, she also had a successful career in banking that included holding executive positions at three local banks. In 2003 and 2009, Zoro was appointed by the Governor to WWU's board of trustees. Later she was elected as president of the WWU Foundation board of directors. She served on the board of directors for the Whatcom Alliance for Healthcare Access, and was president of the St. Luke's Foundation Board (now Chuckanut Health Foundation). Zoro is a past chair of the Bellingham Whatcom Economic Development Council, was named Businessperson of the Year, and received the Whatcom Chamber of Commerce's Woman of the Year award. She was designated a member of the YWCA Northwest Women's Hall of Fame in 2007 where she was lauded as a leader in health and education.

KAREN W. MORSE

b. 1940

Morse will be remembered for her vision for a collaborative community where education always came first.

Dr. Karen W. Morse was president of Western Washington University from 1993 to 2008. She was the second woman in the state's history to lead one of the six publicly-funded colleges and universities and the longest-serving university president in the state. Morse led the state's public four-year institutions in seeking state funding for more faculty, buildings, and programs. Morse said she was proud of "increasing the quality of faculty and students and maintaining a focus on student education in a beautiful environment." Morse, a former chemistry professor, has published widely in her field, holds three patents, and is a fellow of the American Association for the Advancement of Science. She was awarded the Olin-Garvin Medal, the highest award given to a woman for contributions to the field of chemistry. The Chemistry Building at WWU was renamed the Karen W. Morse Hall in 2012. The Karen W. Morse Institute for Leadership was created in September 2009.

PHYLLIS SELF

b. 1937

"In a civilization, it's the arts that last."

Phyllis Self, an accomplished pastel artist and winner of the Mayor's Arts Award, is a patron and champion of the arts in Bellingham. When she and her husband came to Bellingham in 1988, she dedicated herself to the cultural growth of the community. Self joined the board and co-chaired the Mount Baker Theater's fundraising campaign. Restoring the ninety-two-year-old theater, the group transformed it into a grand performing arts center. A decade later, Self stepped up to co-chair the fundraising for the Arts District, which helped finish the theater project and build the Whatcom Museum's Lightcatcher Building where she now serves as a docent. Self became a docent, she said, to become more involved with the museum and cultivate a deeper understanding of art. She co-chaired the Bellingham Arts Commission. Her background includes a therapy practice and leading a hospice grief group.

She was a trustee for Planned Parenthood, the Whatcom Literacy Council, volunteered at Alderwood School and served ten years as a Trustee of Whatcom Community College. She continues to serve on the WCC Foundation Board. The Phyllis and Charles Self Learning Commons on the WCC campus is named for their generous support for the college.

JoAnn Roe-Hubbard

b. 1935

From Castaway Cat to Uncovered City guides, Roe-Hubbard has enjoyed an eclectic writing career.

JoAnn Roe-Hubbard is a life-long journalist who began her career as the staff writer for a University of California at Los Angeles magazine. She is the author of travel articles, children's books, and Pacific Northwest history books. When she moved to Whatcom County in the 1960s, she joined the world tour of sister cities and fell in love with Bellingham's first sister city—Tateyama, Japan. As a member of the Bellingham Sister Cities Association, she helped create a committee to host visitors and educate school children about other countries, for which she received the Japan-America Society President's Award and Washington State Governor's Award. Roe-Hubbard also co-founded the Assistance League of Bellingham whose thrift shop proceeds benefit hospital patient care and provide resources and scholarships for area school children. A prolific writer, she has earned awards from the Pacific Northwest Booksellers, the Photographic Historical Society of N.Y., the National Federation of Press Women, and the Society of American Travel Writers (Western Chapter). Locally, Roe-Hubbard was given the Mayor's Arts Award and was elected to the Northwest Women's Hall of Fame in 2009.

Mary Kay Becker

b. 1946

Becker was first known for her activism in saving the Puget Sound from oil tankers.

Mary Kay Becker moved to Whatcom County in 1969 with a BA from Stanford University. She found work as a paralegal with Northwest Washington Legal Services, and her passion for environmental causes led her into a job as reporter and editor for *Northwest Passage*, a bi-weekly underground newspaper. She was elected to represent the 42nd District in the state legislature from 1975 to 1984, one of the youngest members ever elected. She also co-authored a fictional account of the impact an oil spill would have on the Salish Sea. During that period, she had two children, earned her JD degree from the University of Washington, and established the first all-women law firm in Whatcom County. Becker sat on the Whatcom County Council from 1984 to 1985, and, in 1991, she participated in Washington's first constitutional re-districting commission, seeing the plan adopted on time and under budget without legal challenges. In 1994, Becker was elected to the Washington Court of Appeals where she won re-election three times before stepping down from the bench in 2018.

CHRIS PAUL

b. 1940

"Having projects to take care of teaches responsibility, passion and working together as a family. It teaches work ethic."

Dairy farmer Chris Paul has been a local leader in 4-H and the Future Farmers of American (FFA). Youth programs motivated her, along with other 4-H leaders, to start the Whatcom County Youth Fair. The fair premiered as one of the events in the 1989 Washington State Centennial Celebration. For thirty years, Paul managed and grew the fair into a nonprofit attended by 650 young people, ages six to eighteen. Kids have the opportunity to learn a variety of skills: country crafts, horticulture, knitting, chess strategies, entrepreneurship, and the skills needed to care for and show livestock and domestic animals. People have told her the camp is the most organized camp they have ever seen. In 1997, the Lynden Tribune honored both Paul and Bob Mitchell with the Sol Lewis Award, an award honoring a pair of individuals who have contributed their time, talent, or other resources to improve the local communities. Paul also gives spinning demonstrations at the Jansen Art Center textile studio. She is inspired by the youth of the community because she sees them as the leaders of the next generation.

HARRIET SPANEL

1939–2016

At the request of the neighborhoods, Franklin Park was renamed Harriet Spanel Park in 2017.

Harriet Spanel served in the Washington State 40th District legislature from 1987 to 2009—three terms in the House and four terms in the Senate where she was majority caucus chair for ten years. She grew up in Iowa and graduated as valedictorian of her high school. She earned a mathematics degree from Iowa State University and worked as a computer programmer for the Atomic Energy Commission. In 1968, she and her family moved to Bellingham when her husband began a teaching career at WWU. Spanel was a member of the League of Women Voters, serving many years as president. She was also a member of the Bellingham Planning Commission and the Bellingham Parks and Recreation Board. Spanel said that enrolling in a class at Fairhaven College was "a life-changing experience" that led her to seek political office and fulfill her passion to help her community. Throughout her twenty-two-year political career in Olympia, Spanel worked for the preservation of the environment. The 1,600-acre Harriet Spanel State Forest draws over 100,000 visitors a year and will never be logged.

Catharine (Kitty) Stimpson

1907–1998

Hearing new ideas from her young friends, she would often say, "A fresh breeze is coming through."

Catharine (Kitty) Stimpson was a lifelong resident of Bellingham. Valedictorian of her high school class, she graduated Phi Beta Kappa with an English degree from the University of Washington in 1929. Stimpson was born into a family that believed in service to the community, a creed she exemplified while raising seven children and running her father's real estate and insurance business after his death in 1930. Years later, after her husband's death in 1967, she continued community service and became a nationally-recognized civic leader accruing accolades like "a living treasure" and "Woman of Distinction" and "Citizen of the Year" awards. Health care and education topped her civic concerns, but Stimpson also supported Allied Arts and the Mount Baker Theater. She was a founding trustee of Whatcom Community College and served on the Fairhaven College Advisory Council. In 1977, President Jimmy Carter appointed her to the National Council on Educational Research. A longtime member of St. Luke's hospital board, Stimpson was also appointed to the North Sound Comprehensive Health Planning Council. "Zoe's Garden Wall" in Big Rock Garden was dedicated to Stimpson to honor her community service. Stimpson mentored and generously guided other women and her home was always open to friends, fundraisers, and civic events.

JOAN BEARDSLEY

1942–2007

Joan's smile lit up the room and her enthusiasm for her community was legendary.

Joan Beardsley received a BA in chemistry from Wellesley College in 1964 and a master's degree in science education from Western Washington University in 1986. Having four children of her own convinced her of the importance of teaching. She taught in the Bellingham schools for thirty years, becoming a respected educator. Beardsley was the first chemistry teacher in the state to be nationally board certified, and she won every major science teaching award in the state. She also won the Christa McAuliffe Award for Excellence in Education and was a finalist for the Presidential Award in 1994. Beardsley engaged hundreds of her students in science by having them help with her experiments such as a three-year project to sample soil run-off into Lake Whatcom. Beardsley served on the boards of the Whatcom Land Trust, the American Association of University Women, and the Interfaith Coalition. She sang with the Whatcom Chorale and helped found the Bellingham Music Festival. In 2005, she was elected to the Bellingham City Council after serving five years on the Planning Commission. A scholarship in her name has been established for science and math students at WWU.

LYNDA GOODRICH

b. 1944

"I never thought of myself as a pioneer, but I participated and coached at the beginning of women's sports and Title IX."

Lynda Goodrich may be the most iconic figure in the history of athletics at Western Washington University. A 1962 graduate of Lake Stevens High School, she attended WWU (BA 1966, MA 1973). During her undergraduate years, prior to Title IX (1972), women could only compete in intramural sports. Following five years teaching at West Seattle High School, Goodrich returned to Western to coach women's basketball for nineteen seasons, winning 411 games, and reaching post-season play eighteen times. She was twice a finalist for National Division II Coach of the Year. Goodrich spent twenty-six years as WWU Director of Athletics, an anomaly for a woman at that time. She led the Vikings in winning their first nine national team titles and guided the program's move from the National Association of Intercollegiate Athletics to Division II of the National Collegiate Athletic Association. She added softball and golf as women's varsity sports, but more importantly, Goodrich encouraged academic accomplishment. WWU student

athletes graduated at rates well above the average for NCAA II. Goodrich was inducted into five Halls of Fame and named Vikings Sports Impact Person of the Century (1900-1999). After her 2013 retirement, she received the Division II Athletic Directors Association Lifetime Achievement Award (2014).

Shirley Osterhaus

b. 1946

A sense of fairness drove her to seek justice for the disadvantaged.

S hirley Osterhaus believes being one of ten children, growing up and working together on a farm in Iowa, gave her the sense of fairness and community that has driven her career. Osterhaus received her bachelor's degree at Briar Cliff University and her master's degree from Boston College. She participated in student peace activities during the Vietnam War. Involved with the Franciscan community, she moved to Whatcom County in 1984 to work in Western Washington University's Catholic Campus Ministry. Protesting US involvement in the civil wars of El Salvador and Guatemala led her to found Central American Refugee Assistance, a group whose "underground railway" helped refugees resettle in Canada. After peace accords were signed in 1992, she established an organization promoting the rebuilding of communities ravaged by the war. In 2000, she was fired from campus ministry because of her activism, but was invited to teach at Western's Fairhaven College where, in 2001, she initiated the annual World Issues Forum. Although retired from teaching, Osterhaus is still involved in activism, particularly with the Whatcom Human Rights Task Force which she co-founded in 1994.

NORIKO LAO

1940-2020

"I volunteer with Interfaith Coalition because it provides ways to work alongside people from various faith communities who need a little help."

Noriko Lao has worked and volunteered in both local and global causes. Lao moved from her homeland of Japan to Washington, DC, in 1968 to attend English language school. She spent her career at World Bank, the organization that grants loans to developing countries. She retired as a senior computer analyst and in 1993 moved to Bellingham. Organizations that have benefited from her volunteer efforts to help with homelessness include the Interfaith Coalition, the Opportunity Council, and Lydia Place. She helped construct homes for Habitat for Humanity. She also volunteered as a math tutor at Bellingham Technical College and was the Disaster Team Coordinator at the American Red Cross NW chapter. She served on the Western Jurisdiction Leadership Team of the United Methodist Church and on the National Program Advisory Board of United Methodist Women. Lao has received recognition for her volunteer activities including a US Presidential Pin, a Washington State Governor's Award, the Bishop's Award (from the United Methodist Church), and induction into the Northwest Women's Hall of Fame. She celebrated her eightieth birthday by donating her home to the Interfaith Coalition. After moving to Wesley Homes south of Seattle, intending to continue her volunteer work, Lao died in September 2020.

Juanita Jefferson

b. 1936

"One of the underlying principles we hold dear at Lummi is that all ages need to be represented on important matters."

Lummi tribal leader and civic activist, Juanita Jefferson left her Lummi home as a young child when her father found work with Boeing in Seattle. She too started her career at Boeing, but she began to learn more about her culture from the Seattle Indian Center. She credits the teachers from many tribes at the center for teaching her leadership skills. In time, she was elected president of the Seattle Indian League. Jefferson relocated to the Lummi Nation in 1970 to work as personnel director. She received leadership training at WWU and has served on over forty boards and committees, including the Tribal Council. Working with Lummi youth has been a life-long passion. Jefferson advised the Cedar Project, an adult and youth partnership tasked with ways to make the community safe and to develop opportunities on the reservation. Many of the young people in the program went on to become leaders in the

tribe. In the 1970s, when she felt few people were listening, she focused attention on child sexual abuse, deciding to help one person at a time. The community awakened to the problem, hired a social service director, and began to train tribal members. Now in her eighties, Jefferson is still listening and serving wherever she is needed.

Looking Toward the Future

DORIE BELISLE

b. 1950

Belisle moved to Whatcom County eager to be part of a vibrant agricultural community.

Belisle, raised on a farm in Wisconsin, moved to Whatcom County with her husband, John, and four children in 1995. Using sustainable farming as their philosophy, they developed a 25,000-tree orchard of apples and pears. They began a "Farm to School" program in 2000, expanded the farm to include a store, café, bakery, and distillery, and opened Bellewood Acres to the public in 2002. Over the years, the farm installed a roof runoff management system, drip irrigation, Integrated Pest Management, and planted buffers along Ten Mile Creek's drainage ditches—efforts which earned their sixty-two-acre property the first "Salmon Safe" certification in Washington State. As well as a 1972 BS degree from Minnesota State University, Belisle completed the two-year Washington Agriculture and Forestry Leadership Program and initiated, then managed, the Ten Mile Creek Watershed Project "Neighbor to Neighbor" for eight years. She worked with landowners and several state and local agencies to enhance the land through education and relationship building. In 2019, the Belisles retired from running Bellewood Acres. Belisle continues as a board member of the Salmon Enhancement Association and a member of the Portage Bay Shellfish Protection District Advisory Committee.

Kathi Hiyane-Brown

b. 1951

Though WCC has grown rapidly, it has retained a commitment to personalized instruction and the promotion of success for students of all ages.

D r. Kathi Hiyane-Brown has been the president of Whatcom Community College (WCC) since 2007. She previously served as president of Normandale Community College in Bloomingdale, Minnesota, and as vice president for academic and student affairs at Tacoma Community College. Under her leadership, WCC was added to the list of the top 150 community colleges nationally ranked by the Aspen Institute. WCC became the lead institution of CyberWatch  West, one of only four National Science Foundation-funded centers in the nation dedicated to cybersecurity education. The college is home to the Area Health Education Center for Western Washington, focusing on strengthening health care workforces in underserved communities. The college's grant funding grew from $478,000 to $8.9 million to support the growth in program offerings to serve the community. Hiyane-Brown is a nationally recognized advocate for community colleges, organizational development, and leadership diversity. In addition to her duties as president of WCC, Hiyane-Brown conducts training on leadership and diversity in venues locally, nationally, and internationally. She is committed to supporting leadership development initiatives with underrepresented groups and is a mentor to many aspiring leaders. She was awarded the 2014 Chief Executive Officer award by the Trustees Association of Community and Technical Colleges.

RAQUEL MONTOYA-LEWIS

b. 1968

Bringing a new voice to the Washington Supreme Court.

R aquel Montoya-Lewis was appointed a justice of the Washington Supreme Court in December 2019, the first Native American in the institution's history. Previously, Justice Montoya-Lewis served as a Whatcom County Superior Court judge and presided over Drug Court, an innovative approach to resolving criminal cases collaboratively by address-ing the underlying issues of addiction, mental illness, or homelessness. With experi-ence as a tribal court judge in her native New Mexico, and for the Nooksack Tribe and the Lummi Nation, she served on state and federal advisory committees devel-oping juvenile justice policy, raising issues important to Native Americans and people of color. She also served

as Associate Professor of Law at Fairhaven College of Western Washington University where she created courses on Cultural Identity Development, Transgender Histories and Identities, and Federal Indian Law. She holds a JD degree from the University of Washington School of Law, and a master's degree in social work from the University of New Mexico. Montoya-Lewis is a member of the Pueblos of Isleta and Laguna Indian tribes of New Mexico. Having developed justice systems that reflect the communities in which she has worked, she now brings that voice to the highest court in the state.

KELLI LINVILLE

b. 1948

"It has been a huge honor and a very special experience to be mayor of the town where I was born and raised."

Kelli Linville was Bellingham's first female mayor. A fourth-generation Bellingham resident, she ran several small businesses and served as an educator and a legislator. Linville earned bachelor and master's degrees in speech-language pathology from WWU and worked for sixteen years as a speech pathologist in Bellingham Public Schools. She was president of the Bellingham Education Association in 1989 before entering politics. She was elected to the 42nd district seat of the Washington House of Representatives in 1993, serving seven terms and chairing the House Ways and Means Committee from 2009 to 2010. In 2012, Linville was elected Mayor of Bellingham, and returned to office for a second term in 2015. She ran for mayor under the banner of "relationships, respect, and results," an approach she believes helped her achieve many of her goals—beginning waterfront development, starting a joint lobby team in Olympia with the county and port, chairing the Neighborhood Advisory Committee, developing new parks and bike trails, and stabilizing the biennial budget. She retired in

2019. She shared the Whatcom Dispute Resolution Center's 2014 Peace Builder Award with County Executive Jack Louws. The Northwest Regional Council awarded her the 2010 Legislator of the Year.

SUE SHARPE

b. 1954

Health care and education were central for her work and volunteerism.

Sue Sharpe, former execu-
tive director of the Chuckanut
Health Foundation, has worked
with community-based groups
to improve the health of children
and families in Whatcom County
by using her background in health
care planning and management.
She has served on the Board
of the Northwest Economic
Development Council, Whatcom
Community Foundation, Health
Policy Committee of Whatcom

Alliance for Health Advancement, and the Washington State Health
Insurance Partnership Board. She co-chaired the successful bond
and levy issue to rebuild Bellingham High School and was appointed by Governor Christine Gregoire and later Governor Jay Inslee
to the Western Washington University Board of Trustees. Sharpe
was co-chair of the Insurance Commission Health Care Reform
Realization Committee and Chair of Community Connect. She was
voted Executive of the Year by readers of the Bellingham Business
Journal in 2014 when she was the Executive Director of Chuckanut
Health Foundation (formerly St. Luke's Foundation), which has
granted funding to Bellingham Food Bank, Lighthouse Mission,
Northwest Youth Services, and other community service organizations. She served in that capacity for ten years. Sharpe was inducted into the Northwest Women's Hall of Fame in 2004.

Pat Rose

b. 1945

Rose acquired the skills for her construction company by building her own house.

Pat Rose is a leader in the construction industry of Whatcom County and an active YWCA volunteer, who also served as board president. Shortly after moving to Whatcom County in 1972, Rose became a single parent in need of a job. She was hired at the oil refinery (now Conoco-Phillips), one of the first two women in operations. After five years, she quit to build a house—clearing the land, digging the foundation, framing, and roofing almost entirely by herself. With the skills learned and her refinery experience, Rose went into the construction business, eventually obtaining a general contractor's license and forming Rose Construction in 1986. Before selling the company to her project manager in 2012, she received several building industry awards. She also received recognition for service projects undertaken for the Opportunity Council. Rose's commitment to the community goes beyond construction. Through Girl Scouts of America, she initiated crafts programs for children at migrant farm worker camps and, in the 90s, she engaged in the successful effort to defeat statewide anti-gay initiatives. In retirement, she is still an active YWCA volunteer, directing renovation and maintenance work.

Deborra Garrett

b. 1951

Garrett received the Washington State Bar Association's local hero's award for representing the library's case.

Deborra Garrett was the first woman elected to the bench of the Whatcom County Superior Court. Before moving to Bellingham in 1979, Garrett worked as a trial attorney for the National Labor Relations Board. In her first Bellingham job, she served as an attorney with Evergreen Legal Services, providing legal assistance to indigent individuals. After switching to private practice in employment law in 1989, Garrett represented the plaintiff in a landmark disability rights case, *Kimbro v. Atlantic Richfield Company*, which established standards later encoded in the Americans with Disabilities Act. Representing the Whatcom County Library System in 2004, Garrett successfully argued that confidential use of a public library is protected by the First Amendment, leading the FBI to withdraw their subpoena for library users' lending records. Garrett served on the board of the Womencare Shelter and was an active member of Whatcom County's Incarceration and Prevention and Reduction Task Force. She was a leader in establishing the new pretrial release program for the Superior Court, which helps reduce the number of persons held in jail awaiting trial. Garrett served on the court from 2012 to 2020.

ROSALINDA GUILLEN

b. 1951

Inspired by Cesar Chavez, Guillen seeks justice for farm workers and immigrants.

Rosalinda Guillen has been an activist and farm-worker justice leader for more than thirty years. A passionate organizer and labor activist who wanted to build on the work of Cesar Chavez, she founded the Whatcom County chapter of the National Rainbow Coalition. In 1995, the coalition won the first-ever farm workers' collective bargaining agreement in the state of Washington. Wanting to establish a local real-world model of collective action, in 2004, she founded, and still serves as executive director of, Community to Community Development (C2C) in Whatcom County. C2C is a grassroots organization led by women of color that fights for better farm-working conditions and immigrant rights. The group is instrumental in voter registration and encouraging education in the local farm worker community, with particular focus on women. C2C also puts production into the hands of farm workers through the establishment of worker-owned co-ops, which own the land and sell the harvest. The first such co-op was established in 2017, currently farming sixty-five acres in Whatcom County.

MAURI INGRAM

b. 1963

The Whatcom Community Foundation was founded in 1996 with one purpose: to improve life in our corner of the world.

Mauri Ingram is the president and CEO of the Whatcom Community Foundation. The foundation offers funding opportunities that support nonprofit charitable organizations, public institutions, and tribal members working to help Whatcom County flourish. Ingram grew up in Michigan, earned a business management degree from Towson State University in Maryland and a master's degree in finance and marketing from the University of Washington. After moving to Bellingham, Ingram started and co-owned the Little Cheerful Cafe, the first restaurant in downtown Bellingham to receive a permit

for outdoor dining. She also owned the Calumet restaurant. Ingram founded the Downtown Renaissance Network which later became the Downtown Bellingham Partnership, and served as executive director. She was co-founder of the Northwest Women's Hall of Fame and Leadership Whatcom. Ingram has been active on many local boards including Sustainable Connections and Bellingham City Club and has served as a member of Bellingham's parking commission. She is a skilled raconteur and in demand as a speaker. Her twin girls, adopted from China in 2010, keep her busy but she still manages to travel to statewide meetings for the AFP Advancement Northwest, a statewide association of fundraising professionals.

Flo Simon

b. 1965

"I have enjoyed serving where I live and play. What motivates me is making a difference by helping others."

Flo Simon has been a Washington resident since 1977 when her father was stationed at Fort Lewis. She graduated from North Thurston High School in 1983. Simon attended Ft. Steilacoom Community College and transferred to WWU in 1985 to study business administration. Her passion for helping others led her to pursue a career in law enforcement and, in 1989, she was hired by the Bellingham Police Department, serving in many divisions. In 2000, she was promoted to sergeant and earned promotion to lieutenant in 2006 to oversee the Investigations Division. In 2008, she became deputy chief and currently manages the Operations Division. Simon attended the FBI National Academy in Quantico, Virginia, in 2002 and is dedicated to developing future leaders in

the agency. She is a member of the Bellingham Bay Rotary Club and serves as a board member for the Whatcom Community Foundation and the Bellingham Public School Foundation. Every year, Simon hosts an annual barbeque for the VFW. "I do it because my dad was a veteran and served his country for thirty years," she says. "It's my small way to say thank you for your service."

Janet Marino

b. 1975

"I feel fortunate that I have work that makes a difference in this world."

While a student in WWU's Political Science Department, Marino worked at the RE Store—the retail operation of Re Sources for Sustainable Connections—for seven years. After a year in Olympia, she returned to Bellingham and was hired as the Operations Manager for the YWCA. She credits Julie Foster, former executive director of the YWCA, for helping her spread her wings and learn new skills like grant writing, and cites the importance of mentoring as a means for career advancement. Marino helped pass the first Bellingham Home Fund measure partly because "the most rewarding moment I had at work was to move a resident into her first apartment." In 2011, she became the executive director of the Whatcom Peace and Justice Center and remains on the board today. Coming full circle to her time as a WWU student, she has returned to work at RE Sources as the program director. Marino shows her intricate pen and ink drawings, volunteers at the Stringband Jamboree, and works for various local campaigns. She has sewn hundreds of masks to protect people from COVID-19 and hangs them in her garden for people to pick up.

League of Women Voters

Local Chapter est. 1956

The League believes democracy is not a spectator sport.

The League of Women Voters (LWV) was organized on February 14, 1920, as a "mighty political experiment" aimed to help newly enfranchised women exercise their responsibilities as voters. On March 14, 2020, the League celebrated its 100th birthday. Since 1973, both women and men can be members. LWV operates at the local, state, and national level and is officially nonpartisan—it neither supports nor opposes candidates or parties. After careful study of issues, the league does support and advocate for a variety of progressive public policy positions. On February 14, 1956, four local women—Ina Kirkman, Margaret Joule, Jessie VandeWetering, and Marian Doubt—signed the Articles of Incorporation for the LWV of Bellingham Inc. Over the years, the local league has studied and instituted action on immigration, racial equity, local representative government, climate change, growth management, women's economic security, and deep-water ports. The public is welcome at all League of Women Voters' educational meetings. Today, the LWV of Bellingham/Whatcom County is over 300 members strong. Standing committees work on racial justice, climate change, voting rights, and its core mission—registering voters and holding candidate and issue forums during election season.

PHOTOGRAPH CREDITS

Cover and Chapter Pages: *Whatcom Museum of Art and History, Jeff Jewell Research Technician.*

Aftermath Club, pg 24: *Whatcom Museum of Art and History, Jeff Jewell, Research Technician.*

Anne Brown, pg 33: *Courtesy of Kelly Alyotte.*

Bess Bay, pg 20: *Special Collections Wilson Library WWU, Tamara Belts, Mgr.*

Bess Christman, pg 34: *Special Collections Wilson Library WWU, Tamara Belts. Mgr.*

Carol Batdorf, pg 37: *Whatcom Museum of Art and History. Jeff Jewel, Research Technician.*

Catharine Stimpson, pg 52: *Courtesy of daughter, Susan Trimmingham.*

Catherine May, pg 31: *Whatcom Museum of Art and History, Jeff Jewell, Research Technician.*

Catherine Montgomery, pg 22: *Whatcom Museum of Art and History, Jeff Jewell, Research Technician.*

Catherine Tally, pg 39: *Courtesy of the Oreiro-Tally families.*

Chris Paul, pg 50: *Courtesy photo.*

Clare vg Thomas, pg 30: *Northwest Hall of Fame/YWCA.*

Deborra Garrett, pg 66: *Courtesy of Jill Bernstein.*

Dolly Connelly, pg 23: *Courtesy of son, Joel Connelly.*

Dorie Belize, pg 60: *Nooksack Salmon Enhancement Association (NSEA).*

Dorothy Dale, pg 36: *Courtesy of Donita Reams.*

Ella Higginson, pg 15: *Whatcom Museum of Art and History, Jeff Jewell, Research Technician.*

Flo Simon, pg 69: *Courtesy of Jill Bernstein.*

Frances Axtel, pg 18: *photo # 2004.0.551.72, Washington State Historical Society, Tacoma WA.*

Frances Larrabee, pg 16: *Whatcom Museum of Art and History, Jeff Jewell, Research Technician.*

Harriet Spanel, pg 51: *100 Years of Courage and Change by Lynn Masland.*

Helen Loggie, pg 17: *Whatcom Museum of History and Art, Jeff Jewell, Research Technician.*

Ida Baker, pg 14: *Special Collections Wilson Library WWU, Tamara Belts, Mgr.*

Janet Marino, pg 70: *Courtesy photo.*

Jo Ann Roe-Hubbard, pg 48: *Whatcom Museum of Art and History, Jeff Jewell Research Technician.*

Joan Beardsley, pg 53: *Courtesy of Varya Fish*

Juanita Jefferson, pg 57: *Whatcom Watch, May 2016, James K Jefferson, Photographer.*

Julie Foster, pg 44: *Courtesy of Chuck Foster*

Karen Morse, pg 46: *DIT Special Collections, Wilson Library, WWU, Tamara Belts, Mgr.*

Kathi Hiyane-Brown, pg 61: *Whatcom Community College, Rafeeka Kloke.*

Kelli Linville, pg 63: *Courtesy Photo.*

League of Women Voters, pg 71: *2020 registering voters at Western. Robert Clark, MGF Digital Services WWU.*

Lois Garlick, pg 29: *Center for Pacific Northwest Studies, Ruth Steele.*

Lynda Goodrich, pg 54: *DIT Special Collections, Wilson Library WWU, Tamara Belts, Mgr.*

Mabel Zoe Wilson, pg 19: *Special Collections Wilson Library WWU, Tamara Belts, Mgr.*

Mary Kay Becker, pg 49: *Special Collections Wilson Library WWU, Tamara Belts, Mgr.*

Mary Robinson, pg 32: *Courtesy of Robinson family.*

Mauri Ingram, pg 68: *Courtesy Photo.*

Nellie Brown Duff, pg 21: *Whatcom Museum of Art and History, Jeff Jewell Research Technician.*

Noemi Ban, pg 38: *Ray Wolpow Institute and Steve Ban.*

Noriko Lao, pg 56: *Courtesy of Habitat for Humanity, Whatcom County.*

Pat Rose, pg 65: *Courtesy photo.*

Peggy Zoro, pg 45: *Donor Relations, WWU.*

Phoebe Judson, pg 12: *Whatcom Museum of Art and History, Jeff Jewell, Research Technician.*

Phyllis Self, pg 47: *Courtesy photo.*

Ramona Morris, pg 35: *Courtesy of family.*

Raquel Montoya-Lewis, pg 62: *Courtesy of Jill Bernstein.*

Rosalinde Guillen, pg 67: *Courtesy photo.*

Shirley Osterhaus, pg 55: *Courtesy photo.*

Sisters of St. Joseph, pg 13: *Whatcom Museum of Art and History, Jeff Jewel Research Technician.*

Sue Sharpe, pg 64: *Courtesy of Chuckanut Foundation.*

Violet Hillaire, pg 28: *Courtesy of the Hillaire family.*

YWCA, pg 40: *Whatcom Museum of Art and History, Jeff Jewel, Research Technician.*

BIBLIOGRAPHY

"100 Years of LWV." League of Women Voters, February 14, 1970. https://www.lwv.org/about-us/history.

"About the President." Whatcom Community College. Accessed July 1, 2020. https://www.whatcom.edu/about-the-college/college-leadership/about-the-president.

"About Us." Western Washington University Leadership Institute. Western Washington University. Accessed July 1, 2020. https://leadershipinstitute.wwu.edu/about-us/.

"Aftermath Club Records, 1895-2003." Archives West: Orbis Cascade Alliance. Accessed July 1, 2020. http://archiveswest.orbiscascade.org/ark:/80444/xv55411/.

"A Global Vision: Fairhaven Professor Shirley Osterhaus Lives a Life of Activism." The Western Front. Western Washington University, February 29, 2016. https://www.westernfrontonline.com/2016/02/29/a-global-vision/.

Ancestry. Accessed July 1, 2020. https://www.ancestry.com/.

"Anne W. Brown." Legacy.com, July 14, 2014. https://www.legacy.com/obituaries/bellinghamherald/obituary.aspx?n=anne-w-brown&pid=189589997.

Batdorf, Carol. Northwest Native Harvest. Surrey, B.C., Canada: Hancock House Publishers, 1990.

Bellingham Herald. February 11, 1995.

"Bess R. Christman Obituary." Legacy.com, February 17, 2016. https://www.legacy.com/obituaries/bellinghamherald/obituary-preview.aspx?n=bess-r-christman&pid=177747388&referrer=2057 .

"Bess R. Christman." Westford Funeral Home and Cremation Service. Accessed July 1, 2020. https://www.westfordfuneralhome.com/obituaries/Bess-Christman/.

"Brenda Riseland Awarded Lynda Goodrich Legacy Award." Western Washington University Athletics, September 14, 2014. https://wwuvikings.com/news/2019/9/14/gener-

al-brenda-riseland-awarded-lynda-goodrich-legacy-award.
aspx.

"Broadway Hall - Formally the Aftermath Clubhouse (1300 Broadway Street)." City of Bellingham, WA. Accessed July 1, 2020. https://www.cob.org/services/planning/historic/ buildings/Pages/broadway-hall.aspx.

Brown, Anne. "My Life Has Been an Adventure – 80 Years of Reminiscences." Personal papers.

"Bursting through the Glass Ceiling." BBJToday.com. Bellingham Business Journal, June 20, 2006. https://bbjtoday.com/blog/ bursting-through-the-glass-ceiling/868/.

"Catherine A Selander May (1916-2003)." Find a Grave, March 9, 2003. https://www.findagrave.com/memorial/180388294/ catherine-a-may.

Chaloupka, Amy. "Five Women Artists in the Collection: Helen A. Loggie." The Whatcom Museum. Accessed July 1, 2020. https://www.whatcommuseum.org/ five-women-artists-in-the-collection-helen-a-loggie/.

"Charles "X" Larrabee: Fairhaven Entrepreneur." Fairhaven History, October 5, 2019. https://www.fairhavenhistory.com/ content/characters/cx_larrabee.

"Chemistry Building Renamed for Karen Morse." Western Today. Western Washington University, December 17, 2012. https://westerntoday.wwu.edu/features/ chemistry-building-renamed-for-karen-morse.

Clark, Richard Eugene. "1957." In Sam Hill's Peace Arch: Remembrance of Dreams Past, 142. Bloomington, IN: AuthorHouse, 2006.

Congregation of Sisters of St. Joseph of Peace. Accessed July 1, 2020. http://www.csjp.org/.

"Continuing the Legacy of Leadership." YWCA Bellingham, May 29, 2012. https://www.ywcabellingham.org/550-2/.

"C. X. Larrabee." Wikipedia. Wikimedia Foundation. Accessed July 1, 2020. https://en.wikipedia.org/wiki/C._X._Larrabee.

Dale, Al, Evan M. Knappenberger, and Eric S. Dale. Never a Dull Moment: the Memories of Reverend Dr. Alfred S. Dale, Jr.

Bellingham, WA: Alfred S. Dale, 2012.

Deborra Garrett, interview by Marian Exall, Bellingham, Washington, August 6, 2019.

Dewitt, Susan. "We Carry On the Healing." PeaceHealth. Accessed July 1, 2020. https://www.peacehealth.org/sites/default/files/ph_wecarryonhealing_final.pdf.

Dottie Dale and son, interview by Donita Reams and Laurie Hoyt, Bellingham, Washington. September 18, 2019.

Dougherty, Phil. "Axtell, Frances (1866-1953)." The Free Online Encyclopedia of Washington State History - HistoryLink.org, October 27, 2010. https://www.historylink.org/File/9625.

Dougherty, Phil. "Higginson, Ella Rhoads (1862?-1940)." The Free Online Encyclopedia of Washington State History - HistoryLink.org, February 18, 2015. https://www.historylink.org/File/11028.

Dougherty, Phil. "Judson, Phoebe (1831-1926)." The Free Online Encyclopedia of Washington State History - HistoryLink.org, January 17, 2008. https://www.historylink.org/File/8389.

Dougherty, Phil. "Larrabee State Park (Whatcom County)." The Free Online Encyclopedia of Washington State History - HistoryLink.org, July 4, 2011. https://www.historylink.org/File/9861.

"Ella Higginson." Poetry Foundation. Accessed July 1, 2020. https://www.poetryfoundation.org/poets/ella-higginson.

"Environmental Heroes Award Banquet." RE Sources. Accessed July 1, 2020. http://www.re-sources.org/environmentalheroes/past-heroes.

Evelyn Ames, interview by Marian Exall, Bellingham, Washington, August 2019.

"Family Farmers' Restoration Work Breathes New Life into Whatcom County's Four Mile Creek." REAL ENVIRONMENTAL ACTION & LEADERSHIP, May 8, 2018. https://www.farmers-forreal.org/news/family-farmers-restoration-work-breathes-new-life-into-whatcom-countys-four-mile-creek.

Fentress, Kathryn. "Juanita Jefferson: Lummi Elder and Activist." Whatcom Watch Online, May 2016.

https://whatcomwatch.org/index.php/article/
juanita-jefferson-lummi-elder-and-activist/.

Fraley, Zoe, and Lance Henderson. "YWCA Northwest Women's Hall
of Fame to Induct Four." bellinghamherald.com. Bellingham
Herald, March 25, 2007. https://www.bellinghamherald.
com/living/article22195323.html.

"Frances Payne Larrabee: Enriching a Community." Fairhaven
History, October 5, 2019. http://www.fairhavenhistory.com/
content/characters/frances_larrabee.

Freudenberger, Jayne. Email correspondence with Raffeka Kloke,
August 2019.

Funeral Notices. Accessed July 1, 2020. http://wagenweb.org/
whatcom/wgsobits/deathsadc_ales.htm.

"Genrel Lynda Goodrich 116208 Html." Western Washington
University Athletics, May 23, 2018. https://wwuvikings.com/
sports/2018/5/23/genrel-lynda-goodrich-116208-html.
aspx.

"Goodrich Retires after Four-Decade Career at WWU."
Western Washington University, May 6, 2013.
https://westerntoday.wwu.edu/features/
goodrich-retires-after-four-decade-career-at-wwu.

Green Acres Memorial Park (Ferndale, Washington), Bess Bay
headstone.

Harbert, Jessica. "Whatcom County Youth Fair
Celebrates 25 Years." Grow Northwest, April 3,
2013. http://grownorthwest.com/2013/04/
whatcom-county-youth-fair-celebrates-25-years/.

"Harriet Spanel Obituary." Legacy.com, March 28, 2017.
https://www.legacy.com/obituaries/name/
harriet-spanel-obituary?pid=177616157.

"Healthcare Conversion Foundation CEO Virtual Roundtable: Sue
Sharpe." Philanthropy Northwest. Accessed July 1, 2020.
https://philanthropynw.org/healthcare-conversion-founda-
tion-ceo-virtual-roundtable-sue-sharpe.

Heath, Wallace G., Maxwell C. King, and Robert T. Patton. Lummi
Aquaculture: Final Report to the Economic Development
Administration, U.S. Department of Commerce, Technical

Assistance Grant No.07-6-09226-2. Lummi Indian Business Council, 1975.

Hewitt, Sally. "A Legacy of Civic Involvement: Remembering Lois Garlick." Whatcom Watch Online, August 2015. http://www.whatcomwatch.org/php/WW_open.php?id=1899.

Higginson, Ella. Selected Writings of Ella Higginson: Inventing Pacific Northwest Literature. Edited by Laura Laffrado. Bellingham, WA: Whatcom County Historical Society, 2015.

"Holocaust and Genocide Studies Minor." The Ray Wolpow Institute. Western Washington University. Accessed July 1, 2020. https://rwi.wwu.edu/hgst-minor/.

"Holocaust Survivor Noémi Ban Dies at 96." bellinghamherald.com. Bellingham Herald, June 9, 2019. https://www.bellingham-herald.com/news/local/article231367853.html.

Hormal, Elaine. Letter to Chris Paul, 2019.

"Howard Harris Lifetime Peacemaker Award." Whatcom Peace & Justice Center. Accessed July 1, 2020. https://www.whatcom-pjc.org/howard-harris-lifetime-peacemaker-award.html.

Hsu, Judy Chia Hui. "Western Washington University President Retiring." The Seattle Times. The Seattle Times Company, September 22, 2007. https://www.seattletimes.com/seattle-news/education/western-washington-university-president-retiring/.

"Ice Cream Social Will Honor Retired Bellingham Public Health Nurse Anne Brown." Bellingham Herald. 2014.

Internet Archive: Wayback Machine. Accessed July 1, 2020. https://archive.org/web/.

Janet Marino, interview by Jayne Freudenberger and Elsie Heinrick, Bellingham,Washington, November 8, 2019.

JoAnn Roe, feature writer, photographer, book author. Accessed July 1, 2020. http://joannroe.com/.

"John Joseph (J.J.) Donovan Building Fairhaven." Fairhaven History, October 5, 2019. https://www.fairhavenhistory.com/content/characters/jj_donovan.

Johnston, Thomas Alix, and Dorothy Koert. Beyond the Veil: the

Etchings of Helen Loggie. Whatcom Museum of History and Art, 1979.

Journal of the Whatcom County Historical Society, no. 6 (December 2005). See notes below

Juanita Jefferson, telephone interview by Jayne Freudenberger. November 2019.

"Julie D. Foster." Legacy.com, October 16, 2016. https://www. legacy.com/obituaries/bellinghamherald/obituary. aspx?n=julie-d-foster&pid=182160182.

Kahn, Dean. "Former Sen. Spanel Remembered as Effective, 'Authentic' Leader." bellinghamherald.com. Bellingham Herald, February 3, 2016. https://www.bellinghamherald. com/news/local/article58140303.html.

Kahn, Dean. "Ice Cream Social Will Honor Retired Bellingham Public Health Nurse Anne Brown." bellinghamherald.com. Bellingham Herald, September 2, 2014. https://www.belling- hamherald.com/news/local/article22245207.html.

Kahn, Dean. "Lois Garlick, Whatcom Environmental Leader, Dies at 95." bellinghamherald.com. Bellingham Herald, July 2, 2015. https://www.bellinghamherald.com/news/local/arti- cle26059501.html.

Kirschner, Kate. Email correspondence with Joel Connelly, 2019.

Kershner, Kate. "Connelly, Dolly (1913-1995)." HistoryLink.org, August 20, 2011. https://www.historylink.org/File/9890.

Koert, Dorothy. "Helen A. Loggie and her Art." Unpublished manu- script, 1996

Koert, Dorothy. Portrait of Lynden. Lynden Tribune, 1976.

"Leadership Team." Community to Community Development. Accessed July 1, 2020. http://www.foodjustice.org/team.

"League of Women Voters." Wikipedia. Wikimedia Foundation. Accessed July 1, 2020. https://en.wikipedia.org/wiki/ League_of_Women_Voters.

Lynden Tribune. Lynden Tribune. Accessed July 1, 2020. https:// www.lyndentribune.com/.

Mann, Barney "Scout". "Where the Pacific Crest Trail Begins: Is It
    Campo? Manning Park? No, It's Montgomery." Pacific Crest
    Trail Communicator, March 2011. https://www.pcta.org/
    wp-content/uploads/2012/10/Montgomery_March11.pdf.

Marczynski, Evan. "Executive of the Year: Sue Sharpe, Chuckanut
    Health Foundation." BBJToday.com. Bellingham Business
    Journal, May 6, 2014. http://bbjtoday.com/blog/executive-of-
    the-year-sue-sharpe-chuckanut-health-foundation/28071/.

Mary Kay Becker, interview by Marian Exall, Bellingham,
    Washington, August 5, 2019.

Mary Robinson, interview by James Scott, July 28, 1993. Bellingham
    Centennial Oral History Project Records, Center for Pacific
    Northwest Studies, Heritage Resources, Western Washington
    University, Bellingham WA 98225-9123.

Mary Robinson, interview by Kathryn Anderson, July 23, 1996.
    Bellingham Centennial Oral History Project Records, Center
    for Pacific Northwest Studies, Heritage Resources, Western
    Washington University, Bellingham WA 98225-9123.

Masland, Lynne. 100 Years of Challenge and Change: Whatcom
    Women and the Bellingham YWCA. Bellingham: Bellingham
    YWCA, 2008.

Matt Christman and Maureen Christman (children of Bess
    Christman), email correspondence with Donita Reams,
    Bellingham,Washington, July 2019.

Mauri Ingram, interview by Jane Lowrey, Bellingham,Washington,
    July 2019.

"Mayor Kelli Linville Discusses the State of the City." Mt. Baker
    Chapter of the Society for Human Resource Management,
    January 2015. https://mtbakershrm.shrm.org/
    events/2015/01/mayor-kelli-linville-discusses-state-city.

"Mayor Seth Fleetwood Biography." City of Bellingham, WA.
    Accessed July 1, 2020. https://www.cob.org/gov/mayor/
    pages/bio.aspx.

"Meet the Mother of the Pacific Crest Trail: Catherine
    Montgomery." Pacific Crest Trail Association,
    March 8, 2018. https://www.pcta.org/2017/
    mother-pacific-crest-trail-catherine-montgomery-48060/.

NCJFCJ: National Council of Juvenile and Family Court Judges. Accessed July 1, 2020. http://www.ncjfcj.org/.

"Nellie Browne Duff Papers, circa 1859-1970." Archives West: Orbis Cascade Alliance. Accessed July 1, 2020. http://archiveswest. orbiscascade.org/ark:/80444/xv71774.

"Nellie Browne Duff." SangamonLink, May 5, 2015. http://sangamoncountyhistory.org/wp/?p=2339.

"Noemi Ban." Legacy.com, May 11, 2019. https://www. legacy.com/obituaries/bellinghamherald/obituary. aspx?n=noemi-ban&pid=193115167.

"Noémi Ban: Survivor Encyclopedia." Holocaust Center for Humanity. Accessed July 1, 2020. https://holocaustcenterseattle.org/noemi-ban.

Northwest Portland Area Indian Health Board. Accessed July 1, 2020. http://www.npaihb.org/.

"Open House Celebrates 'Lucky' Nurse." Bellingham Herald. September 28, 2006.

"Oral History Interview with Anne Brown, 2006." Archives West: Orbis Cascade Alliance. Accessed July 1, 2020. http://archiveswest.orbiscascade.org/ark:/80444/xv11166.

O'Sullivan, Joseph. "Inslee Appoints Raquel Montoya-Lewis as First Native American to Sit on Washington Supreme Court." The Seattle Times. The Seattle Times Company, December 4, 2019. https://www.seattletimes.com/seattle-news/politics/ inslee-appoints-raquel-montoya-lewis-as-first-native-american-to-sit-on-washington-supreme-court/.

"Our Roots." Sisters of St. Joseph of Peace. Sisters of St. Joseph of Peace. Accessed July 1, 2020. https://csjp.org/about-us/ our-roots/.

Pat Rose, interview by Marian Exall, Bellingham,Washington, August 30, 2019.

"Peggy Zoro." LinkedIn. Accessed July 1, 2020. https://www.linkedin.com/in/peggy-zoro-6887aa10/.

Petruzzi, Tom. "Larrabee, Frances Payne (1867-1941)." The Free Online Encyclopedia of Washington State History - HistoryLink.org, May 11, 2008. https://www.historylink.org/

File/8603.

Phyllis Self, interview by Jayne Freudenberger, Bellingham,Washington, December 2019.

"Ramona Elizabeth Morris." Moles Farewell Tributes & Crematory. Accessed July 1, 2020. https://www.molesfarewelltributes. com/obituaries/ramona-elizabeth-morris/.

"Raquel Montoya-Lewis." Ballotpedia. Accessed July 1, 2020. https://ballotpedia.org/Raquel_Montoya-Lewis.

Raquel Montoya-Lewis, interview by Marian Exall, Bellingham,Washington, July 21, 2019.

Redtfeldt, Colton. "5 Women Artists in the Whatcom Museum's Collection: Ella Higginson." The Whatcom Museum, October 15, 2019. https://www.whatcommuseum. org/5-women-artists-ella-higginson/.

"Remembering Ida Agnes Baker." WWU Heritage Resources, November 6, 2015. https://wwuheri- tageresources.tumblr.com/post/132683081950/ remembering-ida-agnes-baker-born-on-this-day-in.

Rosalinda Guillen, interview by Judith Wiseman, Bellingham, Washington, September 2019.

"Rosalinda Guillen: Rainbow Coalition; United Farm Workers (UFW); LUPE; Community to Community Development (C2C)." Seattle Civil Right and Labor History Project. Accessed July 1, 2020. https://depts.washington.edu/civilr/guillen. htm.

Roth, Lottie Roeder, ed. History of Whatcom County Washington. Vol. 1. Chicago-Seattle: Pioneer Historical Publishing Company, 1926.

Saettone, Gina. "Bellewood Acres Distillery." Edible Seattle, September 21, 2014. https://edibleseattle.com/explore/ artisans/fruit-distilling/.

Sangamon County Historical Society. Accessed July 1, 2020. https://www.sancohis.org/.

Servais, John. "Harriet Spanel Has Passed On." Northwest Citizen. Northwest Citizen, February 3, 2016. https://nwcitizen.com/ entry/harriet-spanel-has-passed-on/category/C28.

Servais, John. "Lois Garlick Was Our Hero." Northwest Citizen. Northwest Citizen, July 9, 2015. https://nwcitizen.com/entry/lois-garlick-was-our-hero.

Shirley Osterhaus, interview by Marian Exall, Bellingham, Washington, July 23, 2019.

Sledge, Stacee. "Lynden Celebrates 125 Years and 'Mother of Lynden,' Phoebe Judson." WhatcomTalk, March 19, 2016. https://www.whatcomtalk.com/2016/03/14/phoebe-judson-mother-of-lynden/.

"Stimpson Family Papers, 1866-1998." Archives West: Orbis Cascade Alliance, n.d. Accessed July 1, 2020.

"Stories of Progress: Building Support for Salmon and Watershed Health Neighbor to Neighbor." Shared Strategy for Puget Sound. Accessed July 1, 2020. https://www.psp.wa.gov/shared-salmon-strategy/progress/progress-building-support.htm.

"Sue Sharpe." Sue Sharpe | Board of Trustees. Western Washington University. Accessed July 1, 2020. https://trustees.wwu.edu/sue-sharpe.

"Superior Court." Whatcom County, WA. Accessed July 1, 2020. http://www.co.whatcom.wa.us/413/superior-court.

Susan Trimingham, daughter of Catharine Stimpson, interview by Judith Weisman, Bellingham, Washington. September 2019.

"Tenmile Treasures." Whatcom Conservation District, 2006. https://www.whatcomcd.org/sites/default/files/publications/tenmile/2006Summer.pdf.

Thompson, John. "Holocaust Survivor Noémi Ban, Community Educator and Outspoken Fixture on Western's Campus for Years, Dies at Age 96." Western Today. Western Washington University, June 10, 2109. https://westerntoday.wwu.edu/news/holocaust-survivor-no-mi-ban-community-educator-and-outspoken-fixture-on-western-s-campus-for.

Tim Douglas, interview by Jayne Freudenberger, Bellingham, Washington. August 2019.

Tim Douglas, interview by Marian Exall, Bellingham, Washington. August 2019.

Tony Hillaire, Tahnee Kawakone, Katrina Rodriguez (descendants of Violet Hillaire), interview by Linda Lambert, Lummi Reservation, August 2019.

"United Way Considers Policy Change," Bellingham Herald, October 31, 2000.

Washington Courts. Accessed July 1, 2020. http://www.courts.wa.gov/.

Washington State Historical Society. Accessed July 1, 2020. http://www.washingtonhistory.org/.

Washington State Legislature. Accessed July 1, 2020. http://www.leg.wa.gov/.

Wechsler, Terry. "Spills and Chills in Print." Whatcom Watch Online, July 2016. https://whatcomwatch.org/index.php/article/spills-and-chills-in-print/.

Westford Funeral Home and Cremation Services. Accessed July 1, 2020. https://www.westfordfuneralhome.com/.

Whatcom County, WA - Official Website. Accessed July 1, 2020. http://www.whatcomcounty.us/.

Whatcom County Youth Fair 2020. Accessed July 1, 2020. https://whatcomcountyyouthfair.org/.

"Wilson Nominates Woman for Board." New York Times. January 6, 1918.

Window on Western 2, no. 1 (1995): 15–15.

"Women of Library History: Mabel Zoe Wilson." Western Today. Western Washington University, March 22, 2016. https://westerntoday.wwu.edu/inthemedia/women-of-library-history-mabel-zoe-wilson.

Young, Elizabeth. "Catherine Montgomery." Badass Womxn in the Pacific Northwest. University of Washington Bothell and University of Washington Libraries, June 10, 2019. https://uw.pressbooks.pub/badasswomxninthepnw/chapter/catherine-montgomery/.

"YWCA Bellingham." YWCA Bellingham - JULIE FOSTER August 27, 1945 – October 23, 2016. Facebook, October 26, 2016. https://www.facebook.com/ywcabellingham/photos/a.147702375247379/1590507217633547/?type=3.